Robert Oppenheimer

The Prometheus biography

The Extraordinary Life and Legacy of the Father

of the Atomic Bomb

Scribe Paradise

Table of contents

Introduction: The Enigma of J. Robert Oppenheimer

Within the vast tapestry of scientific history, there exists a select group of individuals whose enigmatic nature and profound impact on the world stand unparalleled. Amongst these luminaries, one name reigns supreme: J. Robert Oppenheimer. Beneath the depths of his penetrating stare and the mask of his unwavering composure, resides a profound intellect that has intricately woven the very tapestry of our existence.

Renowned as the illustrious "father of the atomic bomb," J. Robert Oppenheimer's indelible mark on the realm of science and his pivotal involvement in the monumental Manhattan

Project have been eternally inscribed upon the hallowed annals of history. However, this enigma possesses a depth that surpasses what initially meets the eye. In the intricate tapestry of his existence, brilliance, controversy, and profound ethical dilemmas interwoven seamlessly. In the annals of history, there exists a tale that revolves around the enigmatic figure known as J. Robert Oppenheimer.

A man of extraordinary influence, he possessed the ability to shape the very fabric of human existence, leaving an indelible mark on the trajectory of our collective destiny. Prepare yourself to be utterly enthralled by a mesmerising narrative that weaves together the threads of scientific brilliance, political machinations, and the profound consequences that arise from the decisions of a single individual.

Robert Oppenheimer: The Prometheus biography

Setting the Stage: The World in the Early 20th Century

The dawning of the early 20th century marked a remarkable epoch of unparalleled metamorphosis and upheaval, a juncture where humanity found itself perched upon the edge of an impending era. The era in question was characterised by a whirlwind of technological progress, international strife, and the emergence of formidable individuals who would leave an indelible mark on the tapestry of human events. With the haze of the industrial revolution gradually dissipating and the resounding echoes of World War I still lingering in the collective consciousness, the global stage stood poised to welcome a fresh era of possibilities and prospects.

Amidst the tempestuous era that gripped the world, a figure emerged, destined to etch his name into the annals of history, evoking both reverence and trepidation - none other than J. Robert Oppenheimer. Oppenheimer, hailed as the venerable "father of the atomic bomb," bestowed upon the realm of science an indelible legacy that would irrevocably reshape the trajectory of human history. However, one cannot help but wonder about the identity of this mysterious individual and the series of events that propelled him into a position of immense influence, ultimately leaving an indelible mark on the course of history.

In order to grasp the intricacies of Oppenheimer's narrative, it becomes imperative to immerse ourselves in the very fabric of the era he inhabited - a realm teetering on the precipice of profound transformation and tumultuous upheaval. In the annals of history, the early 20th century stands as a remarkable epoch, characterised by a confluence of groundbreaking innovations and tumultuous global dynamics. It was during this transformative era that the marvel of the automobile and the wonder of the radio emerged, forever altering the fabric of human existence.

Yet, amidst these remarkable advancements, the world grappled with profound geopolitical struggles that shaped the course of nations and tested the resilience of humanity. Thus, the early 20th century became a crucible of progress and turmoil, where the forces of change and upheaval danced in a delicate balance. In the wake of cataclysmic conflicts, the world found itself entangled in the intricate web of consequences. Devastating wars had left scars that ran deep, etching their mark on the collective consciousness of nations. As the dust settled, new ideologies began to emerge, each vying for dominance in the ever-shifting landscape of ideas. It was a time of intellectual ferment, where minds clashed and debated, seeking to shape the future. Amidst this tumultuous backdrop, the clash of global powers reverberated, as nations jockeyed for supremacy and influence. The world stood at a crossroads, its path uncertain, its destiny hanging in the balance.

Chapter 1: Early Years

From Childhood to Academic Brilliance

In the bustling metropolis of New York City, on the twenty-second day of April in the year 1904, a brilliant mind came into this world. This mind belonged to none other than J. Robert Oppenheimer, a man who would go on to leave an indelible mark on history. Born into a lineage of prosperity and creativity, he emerged as the offspring of Julius Seligmann Oppenheimer, a distinguished figure in the realm of textile importation, and Ella Friedman Oppenheimer, a visionary artist wielding her brush with finesse. From a tender age, Oppenheimer displayed an extraordinary intellect, revealing a profound fascination with the realms of science and mathematics. In the bustling metropolis of New York City, he found himself enrolled in the prestigious Ethical Culture School. Within the hallowed halls of this esteemed institution, his academic prowess shone brightly, as he effortlessly excelled in his studies.

In the year 1921, a young and ambitious Oppenheimer embarked upon his academic journey at the prestigious Harvard University, immersing himself in the captivating realm of physics. In the year 1925, he achieved the remarkable distinction of graduating summa cum laude. Having completed his studies at the esteemed Harvard University, Oppenheimer embarked on a journey across the Atlantic to the enchanting land of England. His destination? The renowned Cavendish Laboratory, nestled within the hallowed halls of the University of

Cambridge. Under the esteemed tutelage of Lord Ernest Rutherford, a luminary in the realm of atomic physics, he diligently honed his craft.

In 1927, Oppenheimer made his triumphant return to the shores of the United States, where he embarked upon a new chapter in his illustrious career. With great zeal and a profound passion for the realm of physics, he assumed the esteemed position of a professor at the prestigious University of California, Berkeley. With remarkable swiftness, he ascended the ranks of the scientific community, emerging as a prominent figure in the realm of physics within the nation. He was renowned for his brilliance, exuding an intellectual prowess that captivated all who encountered him. His charisma, a magnetic force that effortlessly drew people towards him, was a testament to his innate charm. Yet, it was his remarkable talent for inspiring his students that truly set him apart. With every word he spoke, he ignited a flame within their hearts, instilling in them a fervent desire to reach for the stars and surpass their own limitations.

The formative years of Oppenheimer's life were imbued with a resplendent brilliance in the realm of academia. He possessed an innate brilliance that set him apart from his peers, effortlessly surpassing all expectations in his academic pursuits. He possessed an innate sense of curiosity and a penchant for independent thought, unafraid to question the established norms and challenge the prevailing status quo. With the passage of time, these remarkable attributes would prove to be invaluable as he assumed the helm of the illustrious Manhattan Project, a groundbreaking endeavour aimed at harnessing the immense power of the atom and ushering in a new era of scientific achievement.

In the formative years of J. Robert Oppenheimer, several pivotal events played a significant role in shaping his trajectory. These key occurrences, which hold great importance in understanding the eminent physicist's journey, are worth exploring.

In the year 1904, a remarkable individual came into existence in the bustling metropolis of New York City. This individual, whose name would later become synonymous with brilliance and innovation, embarked on a journey that would forever shape the course of history. Fast forward to the year 1921, a pivotal moment in this individual's life. After years of diligent pursuit of knowledge, our protagonist emerged from the hallowed halls of Harvard University, adorned with a prestigious degree in the field of physics. This achievement not only showcased their intellectual prowess but also laid the foundation for a future filled with boundless possibilities.

In the year 1925, our protagonist embarked on a journey of intellectual growth and scientific exploration as they enrolled themselves in the prestigious Cavendish Laboratory at the esteemed University of Cambridge. This hallowed institution, known for its rich history and groundbreaking research, provided the perfect backdrop for our protagonist's pursuit of knowledge and understanding. Immersed in an environment teeming with brilliant minds and cutting-edge experiments, they eagerly delved into the world of scientific inquiry, ready to leave their mark on the annals of academia. Little did they know that In the year 1927, our protagonist finds themselves drawn back to the United States, their homeland, with a noble purpose in mind. They embark on a new chapter of their life, taking up the esteemed role of a physics professor at the prestigious University of California, Berkeley. In this hallowed institution of higher learning, they shall impart their vast knowledge and expertise to eager young minds, shaping the future of scientific inquiry and discovery.

The formative years of Oppenheimer served as the bedrock upon which his subsequent accomplishments were built. From a tender age, his passion for the realms of science and mathematics began to blossom. In addition, he acquired the invaluable skill of critical thinking, allowing him to analyse situations with a discerning eye and form his own independent judgments. His possession of such remarkable qualities would prove to be of immense value in the years that lay ahead, as he embarked on the arduous journey of spearheading the renowned Manhattan Project, an ambitious endeavour aimed at the development of the awe-inspiring atomic bomb.

Chapter 2: Shaping Scientific Minds

Oppenheimer's Academic Journey

The early education of Oppenheimer laid a pivotal groundwork, serving as the bedrock upon which his future academic brilliance would be built. Nurtured within the confines of a household that held science and the arts in high regard, he found himself immersed in a captivating realm of intellectual stimulation. Young Robert was fortunate enough to have been born into a family that had achieved considerable success in the realm of textile importing. This prosperity bestowed upon them the means and opportunities to nurture his burgeoning curiosities and passions.

Oppenheimer's formative years were spent at the prestigious Ethical Culture School in the bustling metropolis of New York City. It was within the hallowed halls of this esteemed institution that he was bestowed with a comprehensive education, carefully crafted to cultivate his intellectual faculties and instil in him a deep sense of moral discernment. The curriculum, meticulously designed to foster critical thinking, placed a strong emphasis on the development of ethical principles and a keen awareness of one's social responsibilities. The nurturing embrace of this environment served as a fertile ground for his inquisitive mind, coaxing him to delve deeper into the mysteries of the world and emboldening him to question the very fabric of his surroundings. Oppenheimer's academic pursuits were profoundly influenced by the school's unwavering commitment to fostering independent inquiry and facilitating open discussions. This emphasis, which held great significance, played a pivotal role in shaping his intellectual trajectory.

In the year 1921, young Oppenheimer embarked on a journey that would forever shape his intellectual trajectory - his enrollment at the prestigious Harvard University. As he stepped foot onto the hallowed grounds of this esteemed institution, he was immediately enveloped by an atmosphere teeming with intellectual fervour. It was within this vibrant setting that Oppenheimer's already burning passion for physics was stoked, igniting a flame that would guide him towards unprecedented heights of scientific inquiry. With remarkable swiftness, he emerged as a distinguished scholar, effortlessly surpassing his peers in academic pursuits and exhibiting a profound understanding of intricate scientific principles. His intellectual curiosity was drawn to the realm of theoretical physics, a captivating field that beckoned him with its profound mysteries. Within this realm, he found himself irresistibly enthralled by the groundbreaking contributions of luminaries such as Albert Einstein, Werner Heisenberg, and Niels Bohr.

In the hallowed halls of Harvard, Oppenheimer found himself under the tutelage of none other than Percy Bridgman, a luminary in the realm of physics and a distinguished Nobel laureate. Renowned for his groundbreaking work in high-pressure physics, Bridgman possessed a rare ability to inspire and guide the minds of budding scientists. It was within this esteemed mentorship that Oppenheimer's intellectual journey took flight, as he absorbed the wisdom and encouragement bestowed upon him by this esteemed figure. The influence of Bridgman's guidance proved to be of utmost importance in the development of Oppenheimer's research and teaching methodologies, as it ingrained within him a deep-seated dedication to intellectual rigour and unwavering precision.

Having achieved the pinnacle of academic success at Harvard, graduating summa cum laude in 1925, Oppenheimer's thirst for intellectual growth propelled him to seek new academic horizons beyond the confines of his alma mater. With a determined stride, he made his way to the illustrious Cavendish Laboratory nestled within the venerable University of Cambridge. It was here, amidst the hallowed halls of academia, that he would embark on a transformative journey under the esteemed guidance of none other than Lord Ernest Rutherford himself. A luminary in the realm of atomic physics, Lord Rutherford's pioneering spirit and profound knowledge were renowned far and wide. In this esteemed institution, our protagonist would have the privilege of learning from the very best, as he delved into the intricate complexities of the atomic world. During this pivotal period, Oppenheimer found himself immersed in the captivating realm of quantum mechanics and theoretical physics, a journey that would profoundly shape his intellectual development.

In 1927, Oppenheimer made his way back to the United States, his homeland. With a renewed sense of purpose, he embarked on a new chapter of his life as a member of the esteemed faculty at the University of California, Berkeley. It did not take long for Oppenheimer to make his mark in the academic realm, as he swiftly ascended to the ranks of the most prominent physicists of his time. Renowned for their lucidity, intellectual rigour, and the fervour with which he imparted intricate scientific principles, his lectures stood as a testament to his exceptional prowess as an educator.

With an infectious enthusiasm and undeniable charisma, Oppenheimer became a beacon of inspiration for a burgeoning generation of physicists. His magnetic personality and unwavering passion for the field ignited a fire within these aspiring scientists, propelling them towards their own remarkable achievements. Indeed, many of these bright minds, nurtured under Oppenheimer's tutelage, would later carve their own paths of distinction, leaving an indelible mark on the scientific community.

As Oppenheimer's illustrious academic journey unfolded, his reputation transcended the confines of the scholarly realm. He ascended to the esteemed position of a prominent consultant to the U.S. government, bestowing upon him the opportunity to impart invaluable insights and unparalleled expertise in the realm of nuclear weapons research. In 1942, his immersion in the Manhattan Project served as a profound testament to his exceptional leadership prowess and remarkable scientific acumen.

In the midst of the Manhattan Project, it was the indomitable leadership of Oppenheimer that played a pivotal role in orchestrating the harmonious collaboration among a diverse group of brilliant minds, including scientists, engineers, and technicians hailing from a multitude of disciplines. His prowess in leadership shone brilliantly as he deftly navigated the intricate web of challenges that accompanied the project, deftly steering it towards triumph and overseeing the triumphant creation of the world's first atomic bombs.

In the aftermath of the cataclysmic World War II, Oppenheimer, a brilliant mind in the realm of nuclear research, persisted in his unwavering dedication to the advancement of this groundbreaking field. However, as the years unfolded, a profound sense of apprehension began to take root within him, stemming from the ominous spectre of nuclear weapons and their perilous implications. He fervently championed the cause of international controls on nuclear proliferation, placing utmost emphasis on the imperative of responsible utilisation and the relentless pursuit of global peace.

Oppenheimer's academic odyssey was marked by an insatiable thirst for knowledge and an unwavering dedication to pushing the boundaries of scientific understanding. With a mind that sparkled like the stars themselves, his brilliance in the realm of physics was nothing short of awe-inspiring. But it was not just his intellectual prowess that set him apart; it was the way he effortlessly wove together the art of teaching and the art of leadership, creating a tapestry of influence that would forever leave an indelible mark on the scientific community. In addition to his notable scientific accomplishments, it is the profound sense of moral responsibility and unwavering dedication to global security that truly define his extraordinary legacy as a scientist, educator, and forward-thinking luminary.

The enduring impact of Oppenheimer's scientific contributions and his unwavering dedication to promoting peace on the global stage cannot be overstated. With his groundbreaking contributions to the realm of theoretical physics, he not only propelled our comprehension of the fundamental principles that govern the vast expanse of the universe but also forged a path towards a multitude of technological advancements and innovative breakthroughs.

As the dawn of the atomic age emerged, Oppenheimer found himself entangled in the intricate web of profound ethical implications that accompanied the very nuclear weapons he had played a pivotal role in bringing to life. The profound impact of witnessing the cataclysmic might unleashed by the bombs dropped on Hiroshima and Nagasaki during the tumultuous era of World War II left an indelible mark on his soul. The profound impact of this experience etched itself upon the very fabric of his conscience, leaving an indelible mark that would forever shape his worldview. From that moment forward, he emerged as a fervent and vocal champion, tirelessly advocating for the cause of nuclear disarmament and the imperative of arms control.

In the era that followed the war, Oppenheimer, undeterred by the tumultuous times, persisted in his scholarly endeavours. He found himself occupying esteemed roles at prestigious institutions, most notably the Institute for Advanced Study nestled in the quaint town of

Princeton, New Jersey. With unwavering commitment, he devoted himself to the noble pursuit of imparting knowledge and guiding the budding physicists of tomorrow, fostering a fertile ground for the growth and development of brilliant scientific intellects. Throughout the entirety of his existence, his unwavering dedication to disseminating knowledge and fostering a deep-seated thirst for intellectual exploration remained steadfast.

Nonetheless, notwithstanding the invaluable contributions that Oppenheimer made to the realms of science and education, his political convictions and affiliations found themselves subjected to intense scrutiny amidst the tumultuous climate of the Second Red Scare and the era dominated by McCarthyism. Suspicions regarding his loyalty to the United States arose due to his historical affiliations with leftist organisations and his associations with individuals who faced allegations of communist sympathies.

In 1954, a pivotal moment unfolded in the life of J. Robert Oppenheimer, the renowned physicist. It was during this time that his security clearance, a symbol of trust and access to classified information, was abruptly rescinded. The catalyst for this unprecedented event was a highly contentious security hearing, which left Oppenheimer's professional standing hanging in the balance. The repercussions of this decision would reverberate throughout the scientific community and beyond, forever altering the trajectory of Oppenheimer's illustrious career. The occurrence in question draped a sombre veil over his professional trajectory, leaving an indelible mark on his very being. Despite the circumstances, Oppenheimer persevered in his pursuit of advancing theoretical physics, undeterred by the challenges that lay before him. His unwavering dedication and profound intellect ensured that his contributions to the field remained significant, solidifying his position as a revered and influential figure within the scientific community.

In the wake of the security clearance controversy, Oppenheimer's attention shifted towards the realm of academia, where he wholeheartedly immersed himself in the pursuit of knowledge through research and teaching. His contribution to the advancement of quantum electrodynamics, a captivating realm of physics that delves into the intricate interplay between light and matter, cannot be overstated.

In the twilight of his life, Oppenheimer's unwavering dedication to the cause of global harmony and the elimination of nuclear weapons remained steadfast. He emerged as a fervent and dedicated member of various peace organisations, ardently championing the cause of harmonious conflict resolution and the relentless pursuit of global collaboration.

On the fateful day of February 18, 1967, the world bid farewell to the illustrious J. Robert Oppenheimer, a man whose indelible mark on history remains an enduring source of inspiration for scientists, researchers, and proponents of peace across the globe. His existence serves as a poignant testament to the weighty obligations that accompany the pursuit of scientific breakthroughs, underscoring the significance of employing wisdom for the advancement and upliftment of mankind.

In the annals of history, Oppenheimer's name stands as a testament to the convergence of extraordinary scientific acumen and the weighty moral dilemmas that have plagued humanity in the realm of nuclear armament. The narrative he weaves serves as a poignant cautionary tale, a stark reminder that scientists must not only delve into the depths of their research but also cast their gaze upon the wider tapestry of society and the vast expanse of our world. It is a clarion call, urging these intellectual pioneers to ponder the profound implications their work may have on the very fabric of our existence.

In contemplating the life and work of J. Robert Oppenheimer, one is immediately struck by the profound complexities that lie at the heart of his story. His journey serves as a poignant reminder of the intricate tapestry woven by human ambition, scientific progress, and the unwavering pursuit of peace. Oppenheimer's life, like a masterfully crafted novel, unfolds with a captivating blend of triumphs and tribulations.

From his early days as a brilliant young mind, it was evident that he possessed an insatiable thirst for knowledge and a remarkable aptitude for scientific exploration. His intellectual prowess propelled him to the forefront of the scientific community, where he would ultimately leave an indelible mark. Yet, as with any great narrative, Oppenheimer's tale is not without its darker shades. It was during the tumultuous era of World War II that his brilliance found itself entangled in The enduring legacy of this remarkable individual standing as a luminous beacon, casting its inspiring rays upon the path of future generations. It serves as a poignant reminder, a resounding testament to the boundless potential that scientific advancements hold in their hands, capable of moulding our world into a better place.

Yet, it also imparts a solemn lesson, a gentle admonition that resonates deeply within our hearts - the weighty significance of moral responsibility when confronted with transformative discoveries. In our ongoing journey through the complexities of the contemporary era, the profound wisdom gleaned from the life of Oppenheimer continues to resonate, compelling us to exercise wisdom and ingenuity with a delicate balance of empathy, discernment, and an unwavering dedication to fostering unity on a global scale.

Chapter 3: The Manhattan Project:

Leading the Race for the Atomic Bomb

In the annals of history, there exists a moment that stands as a turning point, forever altering the course of events. It was the year 1939 when the seeds of a groundbreaking endeavour were sown, birthing what would come to be known as the Manhattan Project. This ambitious undertaking would thrust the United States and its steadfast allies into an exhilarating race against time, all in pursuit of a weapon of unimaginable power - the atomic bomb. Such was the backdrop of this epochal chapter, unfolding amidst the tumultuous backdrop of World War II. Motivated by an overwhelming dread that Nazi Germany might seize the upper hand in this race, the project evolved into an extraordinary and covert scientific pursuit, characterised by unparalleled ambition and secrecy.

Under the guidance of the illustrious J. Robert Oppenheimer, a luminary in the realm of theoretical physics, the endeavour took shape, giving birth to the Los Alamos Laboratory nestled in the picturesque landscapes of New Mexico. This hallowed ground served as the epicentre for the project's relentless pursuit of research and development. The selection of the location was deliberate, driven by its remote and secluded characteristics. This choice ensured a sanctuary of utmost confidentiality, shielding the experiments from the curious gaze of any potential adversaries.

The magnitude of the Manhattan Project was truly unparalleled, as it brought together a vast assemblage of brilliant minds hailing from various disciplines. Countless scientists, engineers, and an extensive support staff, each with their own unique backgrounds, converged to embark on this monumental endeavour. The assemblage comprised individuals hailing from various corners of the United States, a diverse group that included numerous souls who had sought solace in America, having escaped the harrowing clutches of war-torn Europe. The convergence of their combined expertise, intertwined with a fervent devotion to their nation and a palpable sense of immediacy, established the very foundation upon which an extraordinary level of scientific collaboration would soon unfold.

Nevertheless, the endeavour was accompanied by a staggering cost. The Manhattan Project, a monumental endeavour undertaken by the United States during wartime, was fueled by an extraordinary infusion of funding, reaching a staggering sum in the billions of dollars. In the face of an exorbitant price tag, the government found itself driven by an urgent imperative: to swiftly bring an end to the war and avert any additional loss of life. This unwavering determination compelled them to allocate substantial resources towards the endeavour.

In their arduous pursuit of harnessing the power of the atom, the brilliant minds at Los Alamos encountered a multitude of formidable obstacles. One of the pivotal challenges that arose was the imperative to generate a sufficient quantity of fissile material, be it enriched uranium or plutonium, in order to perpetuate a cascading sequence of reactions and ultimately attain a meticulously controlled nuclear detonation. The attainment of this remarkable feat necessitated the undertaking of groundbreaking research and the application of ingenious engineering techniques, thereby propelling the limits of scientific comprehension to new frontiers.

The intricacies inherent in the design of bombs, coupled with the intricate mechanics underlying nuclear reactions, presented formidable obstacles to overcome. The esteemed scientists of Los Alamos were bestowed with the weighty responsibility of fashioning a bomb capable of deftly harnessing and liberating the prodigious reservoirs of energy ensconced within the atom. The development of intricate triggering mechanisms and precise engineering became imperative in order to guarantee the bomb's efficacy while upholding stringent safety protocols.

On that fateful day, the zenith of the Manhattan Project was reached, as the world bore witness to a momentous event. It was the 16th of July in the year 1945 when the first atomic bomb, shrouded in secrecy under the enigmatic moniker "Trinity," was put to the ultimate test. In the vast expanse of the New Mexico desert, a momentous event unfolded at the hallowed grounds of the Trinity Site. It was here that a test of unprecedented magnitude occurred, forever etching its name in the annals of human history. This pivotal moment marked the dawning of a new era, one that would shape the course of civilization—the birth of the nuclear age. The resounding might of the bomb's detonation served as an undeniable testament, affirming that the project had indeed accomplished its paramount aim.

The utilisation of atomic bombs in the aftermath, targeting the Japanese cities of Hiroshima and Nagasaki, on the dates of August 6 and August 9, 1945, respectively, has endured as an exceedingly contentious choice, etching its place in the annals of history. The bombings, with their unfathomable magnitude, unleashed a wave of unparalleled devastation upon the affected regions. In their wake, tens of thousands of lives were abruptly extinguished, leaving behind a harrowing trail of immediate casualties. Yet, the true extent of the calamity extended far beyond the initial toll, as countless individuals were condemned to endure the enduring afflictions brought forth by the insidious effects of radiation exposure.

The bombings, in their own tragic and devastating way, played a pivotal role in expediting the conclusion of World War II. It is an undeniable fact that Japan, mere days following the harrowing events in Nagasaki, made the difficult decision to surrender. Amidst the ongoing discourse surrounding the employment of atomic bombs, a myriad of voices emerge, each presenting their own perspective on the matter. Those in favour of this controversial measure contend that, when considered within the broader context of the war, it can be deemed justifiable. However, there exists a faction that vehemently opposes this stance, perceiving the decision as nothing short of calamitous, fraught with profound humanitarian and ethical ramifications.

The manifold and expansive legacy of the Manhattan Project extends across numerous dimensions. On the one hand, this remarkable event served as a resounding triumph for the realms of science and technology, showcasing the boundless possibilities that can be achieved through the sheer brilliance of human innovation. However, it brought forth a new age fraught with existential peril, as the advent of nuclear weaponry fundamentally altered the geopolitical terrain and heightened the fervour of the arms race among nations possessing these formidable capabilities.

The profound contemplation and spirited debate surrounding the ethical quandaries engendered by the advancement and utilisation of nuclear armaments persist unabated. The profound ethical considerations that envelop the decision to deploy these immensely destructive weapons serve as a poignant reminder of the utmost significance of conscientious governance and the compelling necessity to avert any potential nuclear conflicts in the future.

The profound comprehension of the cataclysmic potential inherent in nuclear weapons, a revelation that emerged from the momentous endeavour known as the Manhattan Project, instigated an imperative for the establishment of an innovative system of governance. This pressing necessity arose from the unprecedented magnitude of this formidable capability, demanding a novel approach to its management and control. With the conclusion of World War II, a profound shift occurred, unveiling the dawn of the nuclear age. In its wake, a collective realisation emerged, casting a sombre light upon the world's stage - the presence and dissemination of nuclear armaments presented an ominous peril to the very fabric of global security and the destiny of humankind.

In the wake of the war's conclusion, the collective attention underwent a profound shift, transitioning from the relentless pursuit of weapon advancement to a more pressing concern: how to avert the looming spectre of nuclear conflict and establish an enduring guarantee that these devastating instruments would forever remain dormant. Through the diligent pursuit of diplomacy, a remarkable series of endeavours materialised, resulting in the creation of esteemed international entities and accords that were specifically designed to mitigate the perils inherent in the possession and utilisation of nuclear armaments.

In the annals of nuclear governance, few milestones hold as much historical weight and enduring significance as the birth of the United Nations (UN) in the year 1945. Inscribed within the sacred pages of the UN Charter lies a profound principle, one that resonates with the very essence of humanity's collective aspirations - the principle of collective security. This noble concept, meticulously crafted by the minds of visionary diplomats, stands as a testament to our unwavering commitment to seek harmony amidst the tumultuous currents of international relations. At its core, the principle of collective security beckons us to embrace the path of peace, urging us to shun the destructive allure of conflict. It implores us to cast aside the weapons of war and instead wield the tools of dialogue, negotiation, and compromise. For within the hallowed halls of

the United Nations, we find solace In a
momentous display of collective determination,
the esteemed UN General Assembly has
resolutely adopted a series of resolutions, each
bearing the weighty ambition of eliminating the
very existence of nuclear weapons from our
world. With unwavering conviction, these
resolutions also seek to establish sanctuaries of
peace and security through the creation of
nuclear-weapon-free zones. This resounding call
to action, echoing across the hallowed halls of
international diplomacy, serves as a testament to
the unwavering commitment of the global
community towards a future free from the spectre
of nuclear devastation.

In the year 1968, a momentous event unfolded as
the Treaty on the Non-Proliferation of Nuclear
Weapons (NPT) was solemnly signed. This
historic agreement was forged with a noble

purpose in mind - to staunchly halt the proliferation of nuclear weapons and fervently advocate for disarmament.

The establishment of the NPT ushered in a new era of collaboration between nations possessing nuclear weapons and those without, laying down a comprehensive framework that acknowledged the universal right of all countries to harness the power of peaceful nuclear technology. Moreover, it compelled nations in possession of nuclear weapons to actively pursue the noble goal of disarmament, thereby fostering a climate of trust and security on a global scale.

In 1996, a monumental agreement known as the Comprehensive Nuclear-Test-Ban Treaty (CTBT) was embraced by the international community. This treaty, with its noble intentions, aimed to prohibit the occurrence of any nuclear explosive tests, regardless of their purpose, be it military or civilian in nature. Despite the fact that the Comprehensive Nuclear-Test-Ban Treaty (CTBT) has not yet been ratified by all nations, its significance cannot be understated. This international agreement marks a crucial milestone in the pursuit of worldwide nuclear disarmament and the imperative goal of curbing the spread of nuclear weapons.

Furthermore, diligent endeavours have been undertaken at the regional level to establish zones that are devoid of nuclear weaponry in particular regions across the globe. The Treaty of Tlatelolco, an exemplary agreement, came into existence with the noble purpose of establishing a nuclear-weapon-free zone in the enchanting regions of Latin America and the Caribbean. It stands as a testament to the collective commitment of nations to safeguard peace and security in these lands.

Notably, this remarkable initiative has inspired the establishment of similar zones in other corners of the globe, such as the mesmerising South Pacific, captivating Southeast Asia, and the vast expanse of Africa. These zones, born out of a shared vision for a world free from the perils of nuclear weapons, serve as beacons of hope and exemplify the power of international cooperation.

Notwithstanding these valiant endeavours, the realm of nuclear governance remains plagued by persistent challenges. The geopolitical landscape remains profoundly influenced by the presence of nuclear weapons, exerting a significant impact on global dynamics. This enduring reality has engendered apprehension regarding the spread of nuclear capabilities and the looming threat of nuclear terrorism.

The actions and policies of states armed with nuclear weapons hold significant sway over the overarching security landscape, giving rise to profound inquiries regarding the durability of deterrence and the perils associated with inadvertent or deliberate deployment.

Furthermore, with the relentless progression of technology, a plethora of fresh obstacles arise within the domain of nuclear governance. In this ever-evolving world, the realm of cybersecurity poses a formidable challenge, as threats loom ominously on the digital horizon. The relentless march of technological progress has not only brought about remarkable advancements in missile technology but has also bestowed upon us the unsettling prospect of new nuclear-armed states emerging onto the global stage. In the face of such pressing concerns, it becomes imperative for us to maintain an unwavering vigilance and cultivate adaptive responses that can effectively navigate these treacherous waters.

In order to effectively tackle these formidable challenges, it is imperative that we prioritise international cooperation and foster open dialogue. Diplomatic endeavours persist in their tireless pursuit to engage with states possessing nuclear weapons, aiming to initiate fruitful discussions on disarmament. Simultaneously, these efforts strive to fortify the existing nuclear safeguards and verification mechanisms, ensuring their efficacy and reliability. In the realm of nuclear non-proliferation and disarmament, the significance of multilateral forums cannot be overstated. These esteemed platforms, including the Conference on Disarmament, the International Atomic Energy Agency (IAEA), and the UN Security Council, assume pivotal roles in advancing these noble objectives.

The pivotal role of civil society and grassroots movements cannot be understated when it comes to their tireless efforts in championing the cause of nuclear disarmament and raising consciousness about the dire repercussions of nuclear warfare. The tireless endeavours of individuals and organisations alike have served as a catalyst for meaningful public dialogue, igniting a collective consciousness that compels governments to place nuclear risk reduction and arms control at the forefront of their agendas.

The profound teachings derived from the Manhattan Project and the subsequent deployment of atomic bombs stand as a poignant testament to the immense destructive power harboured within nuclear weaponry, thereby instilling within us a resounding sense of urgency to avert any forthcoming nuclear hostilities. The pressing need to avert the utilisation of these weapons has engendered a heightened emphasis on the realms of arms control, non-proliferation, and disarmament initiatives.

In its culmination, the Manhattan Project wrought a profound transformation upon the tapestry of history, forever reshaping the trajectory of humankind. It bestowed upon our species the awe-inspiring ability to harness the boundless potential of nuclear energy, a force that could be wielded for both benevolent and malevolent ends.

The project's legacy has ignited a worldwide dedication to nuclear governance, with a singular focus on mitigating the perils linked to nuclear armaments and averting any potential nuclear confrontations in the future.

In the ongoing pursuit of a safer and more secure future, the world finds itself entangled in a complex web of diplomatic engagement, international agreements, and heightened public awareness. These multifaceted endeavours serve as a testament to the profound responsibilities that come hand in hand with possessing such formidable technology. As global citizens, we are collectively engaged in a relentless struggle to navigate the intricate challenges posed by our own creations, all in the name of safeguarding our shared destiny.

Robert Oppenheimer: The Prometheus biography

61

Chapter 4: The Enigma of Oppenheimer:

Unveiling the Man Behind the Science

The life and character of J. Robert Oppenheimer undeniably embodied a remarkable complexity, one that continues to enthral historians, scientists, and the general public alike. From the earliest of days, the brilliance that would come to define him as a physicist shone through with a resplendent glow. His academic pursuits were nothing short of exceptional, as he effortlessly soared above his peers, leaving them in awe of his intellectual prowess. But it was not just his academic achievements that set him apart; it was his unquenchable thirst for knowledge that truly distinguished him. Like a voracious beast, he devoured every piece of information that crossed his path, leaving no stone unturned in his quest for understanding. With a remarkable display of intellectual brilliance, Oppenheimer's graduation from the prestigious Harvard University at the tender age of 18 served as a captivating prelude to the extraordinary achievements that awaited him.

Following the completion of his doctorate at the esteemed University of Cambridge in 1927, Oppenheimer made his triumphant return to the United States, where he embarked upon a remarkable journey in the realm of academia. Through his esteemed teaching position at the illustrious University of California, Berkeley, he was able to solidify his standing as a preeminent physicist within the nation. The enduring legacy of Oppenheimer lies not only in his profound intellect, but also in the captivating charisma that emanated from him. His mere presence had the power to ignite a flame of inspiration within his students, a flame that would burn brightly for generations to come. Such was the magnitude of his influence that he garnered not just admiration, but deep respect from his fellow physicists and those fortunate enough to be mentored by him.

In the tumultuous era of World War II, it was the indomitable spirit and visionary leadership of J. Robert Oppenheimer that catapulted him to the vanguard of the Manhattan Project. This monumental endeavour, shrouded in secrecy and cloaked in urgency, sought to unravel the enigmatic mysteries of atomic power and pave the way for the creation of the awe-inspiring atomic bomb. Oppenheimer, with his unwavering determination and intellectual prowess, assumed a pivotal role in this historic undertaking, guiding a brilliant team of scientists towards the precipice of scientific breakthrough and forever altering the course of human history. In his capacity as the director of the esteemed Los Alamos Laboratory, he assumed the weighty responsibility of orchestrating a harmonious convergence of exceptional intellects hailing from diverse scientific domains. With unwavering determination, he deftly guided this collective of brilliant minds towards the audacious objective of fashioning an unprecedented marvel - the inaugural atomic bomb, destined to reshape the course of history.

In the annals of history, the fateful events that unfolded at the Trinity Site in July of 1945 stand as a testament to the remarkable achievements of the scientific community. The resounding success of the bomb's testing reverberated through the corridors of academia, casting a radiant glow upon the tireless efforts of those who had dedicated their lives to unravelling the mysteries of the universe. Yet, amidst the jubilation and exultation that permeated the air, a shadow of introspection descended upon one man - Oppenheimer. In the wake of this momentous triumph, he found himself confronted with a profound moral quandary, a weighty burden that threatened to eclipse the brilliance of his scientific triumph. For Oppenheimer, the implications of this newfound power were not lost. The destructive force unleashed upon the world had the potential to reshape the very fabric of existence, forever altering the course of humanity. In the depths of his soul, he grappled with the ethical implications of his creation, torn between the awe-inspiring possibilities it presented and the devastating consequences it could unleash. As the world marvelled at the scientific marvel that had been birthed from the crucible of human ingenuity, Oppenheimer's mind was consumed by a tempest of conflicting emotions.

The triumph As I beheld the awe-inspiring might unleashed by the bomb, a profound sense of disquietude enveloped my being, giving rise to a myriad of unsettling inquiries regarding the far-reaching ramifications of such advanced technology. The bombings of Hiroshima and Nagasaki served as a catalyst, further fueling the flames of his internal struggle. The sheer magnitude of devastation and the unfathomable loss of innocent lives burdened his conscience, leaving an indelible mark on his soul.

During the period following the war, Oppenheimer underwent a notable transformation in his perspective regarding nuclear weapons, which ultimately led him to assume the role of a vocal adversary against the escalating nuclear arms race. With fervent conviction, he made a compelling case for the imperative of exercising restraint in the realm of nuclear testing.

His impassioned plea resonated with the audience, as he eloquently articulated the dire consequences that could ensue if such activities were left unchecked. Undoubtedly, his unwavering stance on the matter reflected a deep-rooted belief in the power of international collaboration to stave off the proliferation of nuclear weapons. His grand vision of a world unburdened by the destructive shackles of nuclear weapons sprouted from the fertile soil of his unwavering concern for the destiny of humanity and his unwavering dedication to the noble cause of universal peace.

Nevertheless, as his dissent began to flourish and his disagreements with government policies gained momentum, the discerning gaze of the authorities fixated upon him during the tumultuous era of McCarthyism. This particular period was characterised by an ardent anti-communist sentiment and an unwavering scrutiny of individuals' political leanings. In the year 1954, a grave accusation befell Oppenheimer, casting a shadow of doubt upon his loyalty and trustworthiness. Following a contentious loyalty hearing, his security clearance was ultimately revoked, leaving him in a state of profound uncertainty and vulnerability. The occurrence had a profound effect on him, leaving an indelible mark on both his personal existence and professional trajectory.

Oppenheimer's enigma resides within the delicate balance between his unparalleled scientific brilliance and the profound inner turmoil he faced when confronted with the moral and ethical ramifications of his groundbreaking endeavours. His profound contributions to the realm of physics were nothing short of revolutionary, propelling humanity's comprehension of the vast cosmos and its underlying principles to unprecedented heights. However, it is important to note that these very accomplishments, which were once hailed as remarkable feats of human ingenuity, tragically became the catalyst for the creation of devastating weapons capable of inflicting unparalleled destruction. Regrettably, it was the utilisation of these advancements that ultimately resulted in the catastrophic events that unfolded in Hiroshima and Nagasaki.

The enduring legacy of this individual persists, igniting fervent debates and prompting profound reflections on the pivotal role that scientists play within society. Their discoveries, while undeniably groundbreaking, have also raised pressing questions about the far-reaching consequences that accompany such advancements. Consequently, there is an urgent call for a judicious and conscientious approach to the governance of scientific progress, ensuring that it remains accountable and responsible in its pursuit of knowledge. The life of Oppenheimer stands as a poignant testament to the intricate interplay between scientific advancement and the weighty burden of moral obligation.

In the grand tapestry of history, the enigma that is J. Robert Oppenheimer emerges as a captivating tale of a brilliant intellect, locked in a relentless struggle with the profound ramifications of his groundbreaking discoveries. It serves as a poignant reminder, echoing through the corridors of time, that the relentless pursuit of knowledge must forever be accompanied by a profound and unwavering contemplation of the potential impact it may unleash upon the delicate fabric of humanity. In his narrative, he weaves together a tapestry that not only warns us of the potential pitfalls of scientific advancement but also ignites a spark of hope within us, urging us to confront the intricate ethical dilemmas that accompany progress. Through his words, we are compelled to join hands and forge a path towards a future that cherishes harmony, empathy, and conscientious ingenuity.

The life of J. Robert Oppenheimer stands as a poignant testament to the intricate interplay between scientific advancement and the weighty burden of moral obligation. In the grand tapestry of history, it was his unparalleled brilliance as a physicist that emerged as a pivotal force, shaping the course of events during the tumultuous era of World War II. With unwavering determination and an insatiable thirst for knowledge, he embarked on a journey that would forever alter the trajectory of human existence. It was within the depths of his mind, where ideas danced like ethereal spectres, that the seeds of a groundbreaking innovation were sown - the atomic bomb. As the world teetered on the precipice of destruction, his intellect illuminated the path towards harnessing the unimaginable power locked within the atom, forever etching his name into the annals of scientific achievement.

Nevertheless, as he bore witness to the unfathomable devastation wrought by the bombs in Hiroshima and Nagasaki, a profound sense of moral quandary began to take hold within him. The weighty ethical implications of his own scientific endeavours now loomed large, casting a shadow over his conscience.

The narrative of Oppenheimer serves as a poignant illustration of the moral quandaries that confront scientists when their breakthroughs possess the potential for both beneficial and detrimental outcomes. The protagonist's odyssey evokes deep contemplation regarding the profound impact scientists have had on shaping the course of history. It also underscores the critical significance of engaging in ethical introspection and exercising responsible judgement when embarking on scientific endeavours.

The impact of his legacy reaches far beyond the confines of scientific and historical domains, reverberating within the ongoing discussions surrounding scientific ethics, the progress of technology, and the conscientious application of knowledge. The life of Oppenheimer serves as a poignant reminder of the imperative for scientists and policymakers to possess a profound sense of moral obligation. It is crucial that the pursuit of scientific advancement remains firmly aligned with the enhancement of the human condition and the safeguarding of our planet's future.

Through the embrace of the invaluable lessons gleaned from Oppenheimer's remarkable odyssey, society can embark upon a noble quest to fashion a world wherein the relentless pursuit of scientific advancement is harmoniously intertwined with an unwavering dedication to the principles of ethics and the betterment of all. By undertaking this endeavour, we have the opportunity to pay homage to the enduring legacy of J. Robert Oppenheimer, a luminary in the realm of scientific exploration. Moreover, our collective efforts will serve as a catalyst for a forthcoming era wherein scientific progress is wielded judiciously and conscientiously, ultimately bestowing its advantages upon the entirety of humanity.

Chapter 5:Moral Dilemmas

Ethical Considerations in the Pursuit of Power

The relentless quest for power is an intricate and morally perplexing undertaking, entailing a delicate dance through a labyrinth of ethical dilemmas that possess the potential to shape the lives of individuals, communities, and the very trajectory of history itself. The irresistible allure of power beckons, for it holds within its grasp the tantalising potential to sway and mould the very fabric of our world. Yet, one must tread with utmost caution in both its pursuit and utilisation, for the consequences of our actions ripple far beyond the confines of our immediate desires.

At the heart of the relentless quest for power lies a profound ethical quandary, one that delves into the very essence of human intentions and aspirations. This perennial inquiry revolves around the fundamental question: What drives those who yearn for power? In order to properly assess the ethical implications of the pursuit of power, it becomes imperative to delve into the intricate depths of human motivation.

When one's ultimate aim revolves around fostering positive change, enhancing the well-being of fellow individuals, or advocating for social justice, the pursuit of power can be perceived as a justifiable endeavour. Nevertheless, when one's motivations are rooted in self-interest, fueled by insatiable greed, or intended to exert dominance over others, a host of ethical considerations inevitably come to the forefront.

At the heart of the ethical exploration surrounding the relentless quest for power lies the very methods employed in its attainment. Engaging in unscrupulous or morally questionable methods in pursuit of a desired result presents profound ethical quandaries. The timeless adage, "the ends justify the means," is frequently evoked to rationalise morally questionable deeds undertaken in the pursuit of a loftier objective. Nevertheless, this concept is riddled with ethical perils, for it possesses the capacity to undermine moral values and unleash dire consequences in the pursuit of perceived advantages.

The notion of "choosing the lesser of two evils" introduces yet another moral conundrum. In the intricate tapestry of leadership, there are moments when those who bear the weight of responsibility find themselves at a crossroads, faced with the unenviable task of making choices that carry the potential to inflict harm upon others. In these trying times, leaders often find themselves entangled in a web of contemplation, wrestling with the weighty decision of selecting between two equally unappealing options.

In the realm of decision-making, it is imperative to engage in a meticulous process of evaluation, one that takes into account the gravity of potential outcomes and the moral responsibility associated with inflicting harm while striving for what is believed to be a higher purpose.

The pursuit of power presents an inherent ethical quandary, one that stems from the very nature of power's concentration. The profound influence wielded by a select few individuals or groups over the vast majority of people gives rise to profound inquiries regarding the principles of fairness, equity, and representation. The profound moral quandaries that arise from the potential for exploitation, oppression, and the manipulation of systems and institutions for personal gain cannot be understated. The intricate and perpetual ethical struggle persists in the quest to find equilibrium between the consolidation of authority and the protection of the rights and welfare of the wider population.

The profound influence one's actions have on others is an imperative ethical contemplation when embarking on the quest for power. In the quest for power, whether pursued by individuals or collectives, the ramifications of their endeavours reverberate through the lives of countless others, leaving an indelible mark that can either uplift or plunge them into despair. Engaging in responsible ethical reflection necessitates a profound contemplation of the welfare, entitlements, and inherent worth of all individuals affected by the relentless pursuit of power, extending beyond the mere objectives of those who seek it.

The utilisation of force is frequently entangled with the relentless pursuit of power. In the realm of armed conflicts, political struggles, and social movements alike, it is imperative that we meticulously assess the ethical ramifications associated with the utilisation of force. The utilisation of force possesses the potential to engender the most grievous of outcomes: the irrevocable loss of life, the profound anguish experienced by humanity, and the enduring repercussions that reverberate throughout the very fabric of affected communities. Therefore, it is imperative that this course of action be viewed as a final option, to be utilised only after careful deliberation regarding its appropriateness and the imperative need to minimise any superfluous detriment.

Those individuals who ascend to positions of power are burdened with a weighty ethical obligation to wield their authority with discernment and in service of the collective welfare. The exercise of authority necessitates the presence of responsibility, openness, and an unyielding dedication to the well-being of both individuals and the broader society. Leaders must possess a profound understanding of the immense influence they possess, and be guided by a steadfast commitment to ethical principles in every facet of their decision-making and subsequent actions.

In summation, the relentless quest for power is an intricate and multifarious undertaking that necessitates deep contemplation of its ethical implications at every juncture. In the realm of power, one must possess a profound sense of ethical introspection, an unwavering commitment to transparency, and an abiding concern for the well-being of others. These qualities are indispensable when it comes to navigating the intricate web of challenges and responsibilities that power bestows upon us. The pursuit of power, with its profound ethical implications, necessitates a profound introspection by both individuals and societies alike. It is imperative that we meticulously contemplate the potential ramifications of our endeavours, ensuring that our quest for power is executed in a manner that not only upholds moral principles but also fosters justice and reveres the rights and well-being of all individuals.

Chapter 6: Post-War Era:

Navigating the Complexities of the Cold War

QaThe period that ensued after the culmination of World War II, commonly referred to as the post-war era, was undeniably characterised by a profound sense of transformation and unpredictability. In the annals of history, a profound spectacle unfolded before the eyes of the world, as two formidable superpowers, namely the United States and the Soviet Union, emerged onto the global stage. Their arrival heralded an era of unparalleled significance, one that would forever alter the trajectory of human affairs. This epoch, aptly christened the Cold War, witnessed a relentless rivalry between these titanic nations, whose clash of ideologies and ambitions would reverberate across continents, leaving an indelible mark on the tapestry of time.

The epoch of the Cold War was marked by a palpable undercurrent of geopolitical tension that reverberated between the United States and the Soviet Union, along with their respective allies. This simmering rivalry ultimately culminated in a profound schism, effectively segregating the world into two distinct factions: the Western Bloc and the Eastern Bloc. While the superpowers skillfully managed to avert direct large-scale confrontations, they instead found themselves entangled in a web of proxy wars, deftly manoeuvring to support conflicting factions in a multitude of regional conflicts.

In the midst of the Cold War, an era marked by intense geopolitical tension, a captivating narrative unfolded - one of an unyielding arms race, with a particular focus on the development of nuclear weaponry. Simultaneously, a captivating space race took centre stage, as the two superpowers vied for supremacy, each determined to leave an indelible mark on the annals of history.

The world found itself ensnared in the inescapable grip of a perpetual dread, as the spectre of nuclear war cast its ominous shadow over the global stage. This ever-present fear, with its chilling tendrils, intricately wove itself into the intricate tapestry of international relations, further complicating an already intricate web of diplomatic intricacies.

The Cold War left an indelible mark on the world, its impact stretching across continents and generations. The consequential outcome was the division of Europe, as the Iron Curtain emerged to separate the Eastern and Western Blocs. In the annals of history, the nuclear age dawned upon humanity, casting its ominous shadow as the two superpowers, locked in a fierce rivalry, found themselves in possession of weapons of unparalleled destructive power. The pervasive influence of communism, meticulously propagated by the Soviet Union, served as a catalyst for simmering conflicts across numerous regions, leaving an indelible mark on the intricate tapestry of global politics.

In the annals of history, the Cold War era, with its icy grip on the world, reached its long-awaited denouement in the year 1991. It was during this pivotal moment that the mighty Soviet Union, once a formidable force on the global stage, crumbled under the weight of its own internal strife, marking the definitive end of an era fraught with tension and uncertainty. Nevertheless, the echoes of its legacy continue to resonate in the present era. The enduring tensions between the United States and Russia continue to cast a shadow over the global stage, serving as a constant reminder of the delicate balance that exists between these two formidable powers.

The spectre of nuclear weapons looms large, evoking a sense of trepidation and apprehension within the international community. The world remains acutely aware of the potential catastrophic consequences that could arise from the misuse or proliferation of these destructive forces. Moreover, the ever-evolving threat of terrorism has emerged as a direct consequence of the policies and strategies that were employed during the Cold War era. The intricate web of alliances, covert operations, and proxy conflicts that characterised this period has left an indelible mark on the geopolitical landscape.

As a result, the face of terrorism has undergone a metamorphosis, adapting to the changing dynamics of the post-Cold War world. In this complex and uncertain global environment, it is imperative for nations to navigate the intricate web of international relations with caution and foresight. The delicate balance of power, the spectre of nuclear weapons, and the evolving threat of terrorism serve as constant reminders of the challenges that lie ahead. Only through astute diplomacy, cooperation,

The leaders who presided over the tumultuous era of the Cold War were confronted with the formidable challenge of maintaining a delicate equilibrium. In the midst of a perilous era, their nations stood at the precipice, burdened with the weighty responsibility of safeguarding their very existence. The looming threat of the formidable superpower cast a shadow over their lands, compelling them to navigate treacherous waters with utmost caution.

Their paramount objective: to shield their nations from the clutches of this rival force, while treading delicately to avert the cataclysmic calamity of nuclear warfare. To successfully navigate through these intricate complexities, one had to master the art of cultivating trust and fostering cooperation with the opposing faction. It was imperative to possess a keen sense of foresight, anticipating their every move in order to craft a strategic response that would yield the desired outcome.

Amidst the palpable tension and pervasive uncertainty that permeated the era, it is worth noting that the Cold War served as a catalyst for remarkable advancements and breakthroughs. In the annals of history, it is undeniable that both superpowers, with their unwavering determination, forged ahead on the path of scientific and technological progress.

Their tireless efforts yielded remarkable advancements that left an indelible mark on the world. Moreover, these two formidable forces, in their pursuit of greatness, assumed the mantle of champions for democracy and human rights, using their influence to shape the global stage in a profound manner.

During the tumultuous era of the Cold War, leaders found themselves confronted with a myriad of formidable challenges. These obstacles, both complex and multifaceted, demanded their utmost attention and strategic acumen.

During this tumultuous period, every decision carried the weight of the constant threat of nuclear war.

In the realm of geopolitical dynamics, the arms race emerged as a formidable phenomenon, wherein the two dominant superpowers engaged in a relentless pursuit to construct military forces of unparalleled might. This fervent competition, characterised by an insatiable appetite for resources, not only drained vast reservoirs but also exacerbated the perilous potential for conflict.

The inexorable advance of communism, spearheaded by the Soviet Union's relentless pursuit of global influence, has engendered a series of conflicts that have rendered the task of forging alliances an arduous endeavour for the United States.

The burgeoning significance of the developing world, ensnared in a fierce struggle for dominance between the superpowers, gave birth to a tumultuous era marked by strife and precariousness.

In the realm of clandestine operations and covert endeavours, the art of espionage and intelligence gathering reigns supreme. It is a world shrouded in secrecy, where information is the most coveted currency. From the shadows, skilled operatives navigate treacherous terrain, The era known as the Cold War was marked by a pervasive atmosphere of intrigue, as both superpowers engaged in a complex dance of espionage. With great precision and cunning, they established intricate intelligence networks, meticulously designed to collect vital information and meticulously observe one another's every move.

Spies, those clandestine operatives shrouded in secrecy, were employed with the purpose of acquiring invaluable insights into the intricate realm of military capabilities, the enigmatic realm of political intentions, and the ever-evolving realm of technological advancements. In the pursuit of intellectual supremacy, a captivating saga unfolds, one that is rife with clandestine manoeuvres and the intricate dance of counterintelligence. These covert operations, shrouded in secrecy, cast a shadow of doubt and apprehension over the entire landscape, fostering an atmosphere steeped in mistrust and suspicion.

Nuclear proliferation and arms control have long been subjects of great concern and debate in the international community. The potential for the spread of nuclear weapons to more countries raises serious questions about global security and stability. At the same time, efforts to control and limit the proliferation of these weapons have been met with varying intensity. In the midst of the Cold War, the emergence of nuclear weapons took centre stage, forcing leaders to confront the profound ramifications of nuclear proliferation. The inclusion of non-state actors or rogue states in the equation of nuclear weapons has introduced an additional stratum of intricacy to the ever-evolving geopolitical panorama. As a result, leaders embarked on a quest to establish arms control agreements, such as the renowned Strategic Arms Limitation Talks (SALT) and the esteemed Anti-Ballistic Missile (ABM) Treaty. Their aim was to deftly navigate the treacherous waters of the nuclear arms race, while simultaneously mitigating the perilous threat of inadvertent or deliberate nuclear confrontation.

In the realm of domestic opposition and public sentiment, a significant factor comes into play. The opinions and stances held by individuals within the nation can have a profound impact on the course of events. It is within this context that the dynamics of domestic opposition and public opinion must be examined. During the tumultuous era of the Cold War, leaders on both sides of the ideological divide, namely the United States and the Soviet Union, grappled with the arduous task of navigating the treacherous waters of public opinion within their respective nations. This formidable challenge demanded a delicate balance between the pursuit of national interests and the need to assuage the concerns and aspirations of their citizenry. In the hearts and minds of the populace, a pervasive sense of trepidation took root, as the looming spectre of a cataclysmic nuclear conflict cast its ominous shadow over their daily lives. This palpable anxiety, born from the ever-present threat of annihilation, fueled a fervent desire among the citizenry for tranquillity and harmony to prevail. Consequently, a groundswell of public opinion emerged, exerting immense pressure upon the powers that be to embark upon a path of peace and embrace concerted efforts aimed at disarmament. Moreover, the weighty allocation of funds towards military endeavours and its repercussions on the realms of social and economic progress were subjects of scrutiny from critics on both ends of the spectrum.

Cultural and ideological conflicts have long been a source of tension and discord within societies. These clashes arise when differing beliefs, values, and practices collide, leading to a clash of worldviews. Such conflicts can be found throughout history, spanning across continents and civilizations. During the tumultuous era of the Cold War, the profound ideological chasm separating capitalism and communism served as a catalyst, further fueling the already simmering tensions between the two opposing camps. In their quest for global influence, the United States and the Soviet Union embarked upon elaborate propaganda campaigns, strategically designed to champion their distinctive ideologies and secure the allegiance of impartial nations. Cultural exchanges, in the form of sports competitions and art exhibitions, were ingeniously employed as instruments to exhibit the perceived supremacy of one system over its counterpart.

Space exploration and the remarkable advancements in technology have become intertwined, captivating the imagination of humanity. The vast expanse of the cosmos beckons us to embark on daring expeditions, pushing the boundaries of our knowledge and capabilities. With each passing year, our understanding of the universe expands, thanks to the relentless The pursuit of space supremacy emerged as a pivotal facet of the Cold War era. In the year 1957, a momentous event took place that would forever alter the course of history. The Soviet Union, with great fanfare and scientific prowess, successfully launched the remarkable satellite known as Sputnik. This extraordinary feat of engineering sent shockwaves throughout the world, igniting a fierce competition between nations in the pursuit of technological supremacy.

In the wake of Sputnik's awe-inspiring launch, both the Soviet Union and the United States embarked on a relentless quest to conquer the vast expanse of space. Each nation, driven by a burning desire to assert their dominance, spared no expense in their endeavours. The race for technological superiority had reached unprecedented heights, as both sides sought to outdo one another in a dazzling display of scientific prowess. With each passing achievement, the stakes grew higher, and the tension between these two superpowers became palpable. The world watched with bated breath as milestones were reached and records shattered.

The conquest of space had become The space race, a captivating chapter in human history, unfolded with profound implications that extended far beyond the realm of military strategy. It served as a dazzling spectacle, illuminating the world stage with a display of unparalleled technological prowess and remarkable scientific achievements.

In the realm of historical discourse, the topic of decolonization and the formation of alliances within the Third World holds a significant place. This pivotal era witnessed the liberation of numerous nations from the shackles of colonial rule, as well as the emergence of alliances among these newly independent states. It is within In the wake of the tumultuous post-war period, a remarkable chapter unfolded in the annals of history, as decolonization movements took centre stage across the vast continents of Asia, Africa, and the Middle East. In the wake of their newfound independence, these nascent nations became the coveted battlegrounds for both superpowers, each vying to extend their sphere of influence. With a strategic eye towards securing alliances, both economic and military aid were generously extended by these global giants. Nevertheless, the presence of competition frequently served as a catalyst for regional conflicts and the emergence of proxy wars within these territories, thereby introducing a layer of intricacy to the realm of international diplomacy. In the realm of organisational dynamics, crisis management stands as a pivotal discipline that necessitates astute decision-making and swift action. When confronted with unforeseen circumstances that threaten the stability and The annals of history bear witness to the Cold War, an era marked by a series of gripping moments that reverberated with tension, pushing the entire world perilously close to the precipice of nuclear annihilation.

The year was 1962, a time when the world teetered on the precipice of nuclear catastrophe. It was during this tumultuous period that the Cuban Missile Crisis unfolded, an event that would forever be etched into the annals of history. At its core, this harrowing episode pitted the United States against the formidable Soviet Union, as they engaged in a high-stakes standoff over the contentious issue of nuclear missile deployment in the Caribbean nation of Cuba. In order to avert the looming spectre of escalation and the dire consequences that could ensue, leaders were compelled to exhibit a remarkable degree of restraint, rationality, and adept crisis management.

In the realm of nuclear weaponry, one cannot underestimate the critical importance of command and control. The intricate web of systems and protocols that govern the operation and deployment of these devastating weapons is a subject of utmost gravity and complexity. The responsibility of overseeing this delicate balance falls upon the shoulders of those entrusted with the The task of retaining dominion over nuclear armaments and guaranteeing their safekeeping and strategic deployment posed a formidable quandary for statesmen and women. Stringent protocols and secure command structures were imperative in order to mitigate the potential dangers posed by accidental launches, miscommunications, or unauthorised use.

The leaders of the Cold War era found themselves perpetually ensnared in the intricate web of challenges, their every move dictated by the delicate balance between preserving stability and upholding the fragile fabric of global order. The potential for catastrophic outcomes loomed large, underscoring the imperative for deft diplomacy, meticulous strategizing, and an unwavering dedication to seeking harmonious resolutions to contentious matters. The invaluable insights gleaned from this epoch persistently shape the trajectory of diplomatic endeavours and the intricate tapestry of global interactions in our contemporary world.

In order to triumph over these formidable challenges, leaders were compelled to make arduous choices and deftly tread the tightrope between safeguarding their own nations and sidestepping calamitous clashes. In order to navigate the intricate web of the Cold War, it was imperative for those involved to cultivate a foundation of trust and foster a spirit of cooperation with their counterparts in the opposing superpower. This delicate task of building bridges between adversaries was not merely a desirable endeavour, but rather an indispensable element in effectively managing the multifaceted challenges that defined this era of geopolitical tension.

The enduring legacy of the Cold War continues to weave a tapestry of complexity and contention, leaving an indelible mark on the fabric of modern geopolitics and international relations. The profound wisdom gained from this era holds within it a treasure trove of enlightenment, capable of illuminating our path through the intricate labyrinth of the 21st century. As we confront the myriad complexities that beset us, from the formidable global obstacles that lie in our wake to the ceaseless pursuit of harmony and equilibrium on a worldwide canvas, the lessons gleaned from this period stand as beacons of guidance and understanding.

Chapter 7: Red Scare and Fallout:

Oppenheimer's Controversial Security Clearance Hearing

J. Robert Oppenheimer's security clearance hearing in 1954 was a defining and contentious moment in his life and legacy. As a brilliant physicist and one of the key figures in the development of the atomic bomb, Oppenheimer's contributions during World War II had earned him respect and recognition. However, his past associations with communist individuals and organisations, as well as his opposition to the development of the hydrogen bomb, made him a subject of suspicion and scrutiny during the height of the Red Scare and the Cold War.

The hearing was conducted by the Atomic Energy Commission (AEC) in response to allegations that Oppenheimer posed a security risk due to his past connections with communist sympathisers. The Red Scare was characterised by widespread fear and paranoia about the infiltration of communist ideology and espionage within the United States. As a result, many individuals in the scientific community and other fields were subjected to investigations and loyalty tests.

The Oppenheimer security clearance hearing was highly publicised and drew intense attention from both the public and the scientific community. He was represented by a team of lawyers who sought to defend his character and loyalty to the United States. Oppenheimer passionately testified in his own defence, denying the allegations against him and emphasising his commitment to his country.

However, despite his efforts, the hearing board of the AEC decided to revoke Oppenheimer's security clearance. The decision was a devastating blow to Oppenheimer and had profound implications for his career. It effectively barred him from further government service and severely damaged his reputation within certain circles.

The hearing was seen as emblematic of the political climate of the time, where suspicions of communist sympathies or affiliations could lead to severe consequences. The tensions between the United States and the Soviet Union during the Cold War added to the urgency of the situation, as both countries engaged in a high-stakes arms race, each possessing nuclear weapons capable of catastrophic destruction.

The Oppenheimer security clearance hearing has remained a subject of debate and controversy over the years. Some argue that Oppenheimer was unfairly targeted and victimised by the government's fear-driven and overzealous approach during the Red Scare. They believe that his contributions to the atomic bomb and dedication to the United States should have outweighed past associations. Others contend that Oppenheimer's opposition to the hydrogen bomb and his past affiliations raised legitimate concerns about his loyalty and potential security risks.

Despite the loss of his security clearance, Oppenheimer continued to work as a scientist and remained a respected figure within the scientific community. He contributed significantly to theoretical physics and academia. While his career in government service came to an end, he maintained his commitment to scientific advancement and continued to inspire future generations of scientists.

The Oppenheimer security clearance hearing serves as a powerful reminder of the dangers of McCarthyism and the Red Scare, where the fear of communism led to the erosion of civil liberties and the infringement on individuals' rights. It highlights the importance of safeguarding civil liberties, even during periods of heightened national security concerns, and underscores the significance of protecting the principles of justice, fairness, and due process.

Ultimately, the Oppenheimer security clearance hearing is a poignant chapter in the history of the

Cold War and serves as a cautionary tale about the ethical complexities and consequences of conflating political ideologies with scientific advancements. It underscores the imperative to preserve the principles of open inquiry, intellectual freedom, and respect for individual rights, even in times of national security challenges.

Chapter 8: Legacy of the Bomb

Impact and Reflections on the Atomic Age

The atomic bomb's impact on the world has been profound, affecting both its physical and psychological aspects. The bombings of Hiroshima and Nagasaki in 1945 resulted in the deaths of hundreds of thousands of people and caused extensive destruction. The use of these weapons marked the beginning of the nuclear age, characterised by heightened global tensions and fears of annihilation.

The physical consequences of the atomic bomb are extensively documented. The blast, heat, and radiation emitted by these weapons lead to instantaneous deaths and long-term health issues. Additionally, the radioactive fallout from nuclear explosions contaminates the environment, making it unsafe for human habitation.

The psychological effects of the atomic bomb are less well-understood but equally significant. The knowledge that such powerful weapons exist and could be deployed at any time has instilled anxiety and fear in many individuals. The fear is further compounded by the era of the Cold War, characterised by intense rivalry and suspicion between the United States and the Soviet Union.

The legacy of the atomic bomb is intricate and multi-faceted. It serves as a stark reminder of the devastating capabilities of technology and underscores the paramount importance of pursuing peace. Furthermore, the atomic bomb has also catalysed the development of new technologies with peaceful applications, representing a glimmer of hope amidst the sombre realities of its destruction.

The atomic bomb has profoundly impacted culture and society, with the fear of nuclear war becoming a recurrent theme in literature, film, and art. It has been used as a metaphor for the destructive potential of unchecked ambition and technological advances.

The discussion about the legacy of the atomic bomb remains ongoing. Some view it as a necessary evil that has effectively deterred large-scale conflicts, while others perceive it as a perilous threat to humanity that must be abolished.

The debate surrounding the legacy of the atomic bomb will likely continue for years to come. Nevertheless, there is no denying its profound effects on the world, both in terms of physical devastation and psychological repercussions. It stands as a sombre reminder of the catastrophic power of technology and the imperative to pursue peace as a cornerstone of global existence.

Here are some of the key impacts of the atomic bomb:

The loss of hundreds of thousands of lives.

The bombings of Hiroshima and Nagasaki led to the deaths of hundreds of thousands of people, with long-term radiation effects still affecting survivors today.

The devastation of cities.

The atomic bombs caused immense destruction in two Japanese cities, Hiroshima and Nagasaki, with significant damage to other areas in Japan.

The commencement of the nuclear age.

The atomic bomb's development marked the dawn of the nuclear age, characterised by escalated global tensions and apprehension about potential annihilation.

The advancement of new technologies.

The research and innovation behind the atomic bomb paved the way for the emergence of new technologies, such as nuclear power and nuclear medicine.

The societal and cultural impact.

The fear of nuclear war has permeated literature, film, and art, with the atomic bomb serving as a metaphor for the dangers of unbridled ambition and technological progress.

The legacy of the atomic bomb remains intricate and diverse, serving as a stark reminder of technology's destructive potential and the utmost significance of seeking peaceful resolutions. It also holds promise as a catalyst for the advancement of peaceful technologies. As debates persist regarding its impact and implications, the atomic bomb's enduring effect on culture, society, and global consciousness remains an ever-present reality.

Chapter 9: Beyond the Bomb:

Oppenheimer's Contributions to Science and Education

J. Robert Oppenheimer is widely recognized for his pivotal contribution to the advancement of the atomic bomb. Nevertheless, his profound impact on the realms of science and education transcends mere boundaries.

Oppenheimer, renowned for his exceptional brilliance in the field of physics, possessed an extensive comprehension of the fundamental laws governing the natural world. His contributions to the fields of quantum mechanics, nuclear physics, and astrophysics were of great significance. Additionally, he played a pivotal role in the development of novel educational programs and institutions, exemplified by his contributions to the establishment of the esteemed Institute for Advanced Study in Princeton, New Jersey.

Within the realm of quantum mechanics, Oppenheimer made significant contributions by formulating the Born-Oppenheimer approximation, a pivotal methodology employed to comprehend the intricate dynamics exhibited by molecules. Additionally, his notable contributions extended to the advancement of quantum field theory, a comprehensive framework encompassing all forces of nature within the realm of quantum mechanics.

Within the realm of nuclear physics, Oppenheimer made significant contributions to the advancement of the theory of nuclear fission. This fundamental process involves the division of an atomic nucleus into two smaller nuclei. Additionally, he made significant contributions to the advancement of the theory of nuclear fusion, a fundamental process in which two atomic nuclei merge to create a more substantial nucleus.

Within the realm of astrophysics, Oppenheimer played a pivotal role in the advancement of the theory surrounding black holes. These enigmatic entities, characterised by their immense mass, possess gravitational fields of such magnitude that even the swiftest of light particles find themselves unable to evade their grasp. In addition, he has made significant contributions to the field of neutron star research, focusing on these highly dense celestial bodies that result from the gravitational collapse of stars.

In addition to his notable scientific contributions, it is worth acknowledging that Oppenheimer possessed exceptional talents as both an educator and a communicator. He possessed the ability to articulate intricate scientific concepts with remarkable clarity and captivation. Furthermore, he ardently championed the peaceful application of scientific knowledge. He held the belief that the application of scientific knowledge should be directed towards enhancing the quality of human existence, rather than causing harm or devastation.

The life and work of Oppenheimer serve as a poignant reminder of the immense power wielded by science, as well as the profound significance of education. He was an exceptional scientist whose profound insights greatly advanced our comprehension of the cosmos. In addition, he possessed an exceptional talent for teaching, serving as a source of inspiration for countless generations of students. The enduring impact of his legacy serves as a constant source of inspiration for individuals across the globe.

Quantum mechanics, a field of study that delves into the fundamental principles governing the behaviour of particles at the atomic and subatomic levels, witnessed a significant milestone with Oppenheimer's groundbreaking contributions to the Born-Oppenheimer approximation. This pivotal advancement greatly enhanced our comprehension of molecular structure. This approximation enables physicists to independently analyse the movement of electrons within a molecule, distinct from the motion of the nuclei. Consequently, it significantly simplifies the process of solving the intricate equations of quantum mechanics.

Nuclear physics is a field of study that focuses on the behaviour and properties of atomic nuclei. The contributions made by Oppenheimer in the field of nuclear fission were of utmost significance in the advancement and eventual realisation of the atomic bomb. He played a crucial role in the calculation of the critical mass of uranium-235, which represents the minimum quantity of uranium-235 required to maintain a sustainable nuclear chain reaction.

Astrophysics is a field of study that focuses on the physics of celestial objects and phenomena in the universe. The contributions made by Oppenheimer in the field of black holes were truly groundbreaking. He emerged as a pioneering physicist who possessed the foresight to acknowledge the plausibility of black holes, subsequently contributing significantly to the advancement of the theoretical framework elucidating their functioning.

Education is a fundamental aspect of personal and professional development. It serves as a cornerstone for acquiring knowledge, skills, and competencies that are essential for Oppenheimer demonstrating a steadfast commitment to the advancement of education, actively contributing to the development of innovative educational programs and institutions. He held the esteemed distinction of being a founding member of the renowned Institute for Advanced Study in Princeton, New Jersey, widely recognized as one of the foremost global hubs for cutting-edge research.

The contributions made by Oppenheimer in the fields of science and education have undeniably left a profound and lasting impact on the global stage. Through his diligent efforts, he has made significant contributions to the expansion of our comprehension of the vast cosmos and the subsequent emergence of groundbreaking technologies that have greatly enhanced our daily existence. He possessed exceptional brilliance in the field of science and was renowned for his prowess as an educator. Even to this day, his enduring legacy serves as a profound source of inspiration for individuals across the globe.

Chapter 10: The Human Prometheus:

Understanding Oppenheimer's Profound Influences

In the realm of human mythology, there exists a figure whose name resonates through the ages: Prometheus, the bringer of fire. This ancient tale has captivated the minds of countless

J. Robert Oppenheimer, a luminary in the field of physics, assumed a pivotal role in the advancement of the atomic bomb. He was a multifaceted and polarising individual, and his life and enduring impact remain subjects of ongoing discourse.

Born into a prosperous Jewish family in the year 1904, J. Robert Oppenheimer's place of birth was none other than the illustrious city of New York. He possessed exceptional academic abilities, culminating in his attainment of a degree from the esteemed Harvard University at the remarkably tender age of 18. Subsequently, he embarked upon his academic pursuit of physics at the esteemed University of Cambridge in England, culminating in the conferral of a doctorate upon him in the year 1927.

Following the successful completion of his doctorate, Oppenheimer embarked on a journey back to the United States, where he assumed the esteemed position of a physics professor at the renowned University of California, Berkeley. With remarkable speed, he ascended to the ranks of the foremost physicists in the nation, ultimately assuming the esteemed position of director at the Los Alamos Laboratory in 1943.

Under the guidance of J. Robert Oppenheimer, the Los Alamos Laboratory successfully spearheaded the development of the atomic bomb. The initial testing of the bomb took place in the state of New Mexico during the month of July in the year 1945. Subsequently, it was deployed against Japan in the month of August in the same year.

Following the conclusion of the war, Oppenheimer emerged as a prominent and outspoken adversary of the nuclear arms race. He presented a compelling argument highlighting the perilous implications of nuclear weapon proliferation on the collective well-being of humanity. Furthermore, he advocated for the imperative implementation of a comprehensive ban on nuclear testing.

In 1954, J. Robert Oppenheimer found himself facing grave accusations from the United States government, who deemed him a potential threat to national security. He underwent a loyalty hearing, which ultimately resulted in the revocation of his security clearance.

The life and legacy of Oppenheimer continue to be subjects of ongoing debate in contemporary discourse. There exists a dichotomy in the perception of this individual, with certain individuals venerating him as a heroic figure who played a pivotal role in the triumph of World War II, while others condemn him as a malevolent force responsible for the development of the atomic bomb.

Undoubtedly, Oppenheimer possessed a multifaceted and enigmatic nature. He was an exceptional scientist who made noteworthy contributions to the field of physics. Additionally, he possessed a profound inner turmoil, grappling with the ethical ramifications of his endeavours.

The narrative surrounding Oppenheimer serves as a poignant cautionary tale, shedding light on the inherent perils that can accompany the relentless pursuit of scientific advancement. This serves as a poignant reminder that even the most brilliant intellects have the potential to be harnessed for nefarious ends.

The impact of Oppenheimer's influence has been truly profound. Regarded as one of the preeminent physicists of the 20th century, his contributions have wielded a profound influence on our comprehension of the cosmos. Furthermore, he serves as a poignant symbol, emblematic of the inherent perils associated with nuclear armaments. To this day, his enduring legacy remains a subject of fervent debate and contemplation.

The Prometheus Analogy

The impact of Oppenheimer is evident across various domains. To gain insight into his profound impact, it is instructive to draw a parallel between him and Prometheus, the revered Greek Titan renowned for his audacious act of purloining fire from Zeus and bestowing it upon mankind. Prometheus, in the aftermath of his audacious act of defiance, faced the consequences of his actions. However, his legacy endures as that of a revered hero, for he bestowed upon humanity the invaluable gift of knowledge.

Oppenheimer may be perceived as a contemporary embodiment of Prometheus. He was an exceptional scientist who bestowed upon humanity the formidable capability of harnessing atomic energy for destructive purposes. The bestowed power was not only a blessing, but also a burden. The atomic bomb possesses the capacity to bring about the annihilation of humanity, yet it also harbours the potential to be harnessed for benevolent purposes.

The analogy of Prometheus serves as a poignant reminder that scientific progress, while undeniably transformative, possesses a dual nature, akin to a double-edged sword. The potential applications of this tool are manifold, encompassing both virtuous and malevolent purposes. Ultimately, the responsibility lies with us to deliberate upon and determine the manner in which we shall employ it. The enduring legacy of Oppenheimer serves as a poignant reminder of the imperative to exercise caution when harnessing the immense power of science, and to wield it judiciously and prudently.

The trajectory of nuclear weapons in the coming years

The trajectory of nuclear weapons in the coming years remains uncertain. There exists a divergence of opinions among individuals, with one faction asserting the eventual eradication of their existence, while another faction maintains their perpetual menace to humanity. The enduring legacy of Oppenheimer serves as a poignant reminder that the gravity of the nuclear weapons threat should never be underestimated. It is imperative that we diligently strive to avert the utilisation of these weapons, while concurrently exploring viable means to achieve global disarmament.

The enduring impact of Oppenheimer's influence is poised to resonate for numerous years into the future. He possessed exceptional brilliance as a scientist, embodying a multifaceted and enigmatic persona that served as a poignant symbol of the perils associated with the advancement of scientific knowledge. The enduring legacy of his work serves as a poignant reminder of the imperative to exercise caution when harnessing the immense power of science, emphasising the critical importance of employing it judiciously and with great care.

Conclusion: A Life of Contradictions

Robert Oppenheimer's Enduring Legacy

The life of J. Robert Oppenheimer is a captivating tale that encompasses brilliance, achievements, ethical quandaries, and the intricate interplay between scientific advancement and moral duty. With his notable contributions to the advancement of the atomic bomb during the course of World War II, he solidified his standing as one of the foremost physicists of his era. Nevertheless, his participation in such a revolutionary and devastating endeavour left him wrestling with the profound ethical ramifications of his actions.

The legacy of Oppenheimer stands as a timeless narrative of contradictions, serving as a poignant testament to the intricate interplay between scientific progress and ethical obligations. On the one hand, his exceptional brilliance and unwavering commitment to scientific exploration propelled the limits of human comprehension and laid the foundation for revolutionary technologies and advancements. However, the profound ramifications of the atomic bomb's destructive power gave rise to significant ethical inquiries regarding the utilisation and repercussions of scientific advancement.

Oppenheimer, a figure of great complexity and controversy, experienced pivotal moments throughout his life that left a lasting impact on his trajectory. One such significant event was his security clearance hearing in 1954. The hearing, which emerged as a consequence of the Red Scare and the Cold War, inflicted a significant setback upon his government career, thereby exemplifying the delicate equilibrium between national security imperatives and the protection of civil liberties. In the face of numerous challenges, Oppenheimer tenaciously pursued his scientific endeavours, emerging as a revered luminary within the scientific community. His unwavering commitment and resilience served as a testament to his unwavering dedication to his chosen vocation.

The legacy of Oppenheimer transcends his scientific accomplishments. The story of his life stands as a poignant testament to the ethical quandaries that emerge when scientific breakthroughs are employed for pursuits that carry the potential for catastrophic outcomes. The quest for power, specifically in the realm of nuclear armament, highlights the imperative for deep ethical reflection and meticulous examination of the wider consequences of scientific advancement for the human race.

The life he led serves as a testament to the notion that even the most exceptional intellects are not immune to encountering ethical predicaments and dilemmas while striving for knowledge and progress. The choices and decisions made by individuals possessing immense power and intellect possess the inherent capacity to shape the course of history and engender enduring impacts upon the world. The Oppenheimer case serves as a poignant illustration of the intricate equilibrium between human ingenuity and the imperative of ethical responsibility when confronted with scientific   progress   that   carries   profound consequences.

The lasting impact of Oppenheimer serves as a compelling impetus for present and forthcoming cohorts   of   scientists,   policymakers,   and individuals to confront the intricate ethical dilemmas   that   accompany   scientific advancement. This statement underscores the importance of carefully evaluating the potential ramifications of scientific breakthroughs and technological progress, while also prioritising the collective welfare of the entire human race.

The life of J. Robert Oppenheimer encompasses a multifaceted journey characterised by brilliance, complexity, and profound moral introspection. The lasting impact he has left behind serves as a poignant reminder that the quest for knowledge and influence must always be coupled with an unwavering dedication to ethical values and the conscientious exercise of such authority. The narrative of Oppenheimer compels us to contemplate the consequences of our actions and choices, urging us to aspire towards a future in which scientific advancement is driven by a deep dedication to the advancement of humanity and the safeguarding of peace.

Printed in Poland
by Amazon Fulfillment
Poland Sp. z o.o., Wrocław
25 September 2023

77d900c5-1104-4caf-8d24-c4598600817eR01